How to SWIM

a step·by·step guide

Author:
Liz French

Technical consultant:
Fred Kirby
GB and England Coaching Staff

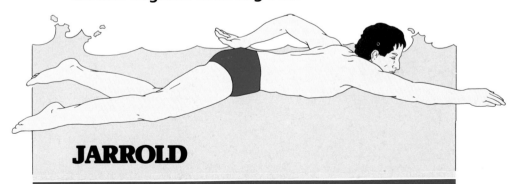

JARROLD

Other titles in this series are:

TENNIS **GOLF**
SQUASH **WINDSURFING**
BADMINTON **SNOOKER**
CROQUET **DINGHY SAILING**
BOWLS **GET FIT FOR SPORT**
TABLE TENNIS

How to SWIM
ISBN 0-7117-0501-1
First published in Great Britain, 1990
Text copyright © Liz French, 1990
This edition copyright © 1990 Jarrold Publishing
Illustrations by Malcolm Ryan

Designed and produced by
Parke Sutton Limited, Norwich
for Jarrold Publishing, Norwich

Contents

Introduction

Swimming requires little or no special equipment. It can be enjoyed equally by young and old alike. And it is the best form of all-round exercise you can take, promoting strength, stamina and flexibility and using every major muscle group in the body. Swimming is also fun! Small wonder, then, that it is the most popular active recreation there is.

'How to Swim' will take you from the basic principles of swimming, through safety precautions and water confidence exercises to good stroke techniques. Of course, there is no substitute for being in the water, and lessons from a qualified teacher are strongly advised. But in the pages that follow you will find invaluable advice that will help you acquire confidence in your strokes and give you useful hints for effective practising.

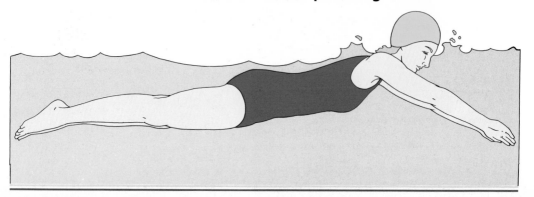

Once you have mastered the basic strokes, or even while you are learning, it is a good idea to join a swimming club. Clubs often welcome beginners — there are some clubs especially for adult learners — and can offer much more than just the company of others. There may be competitions and special events, for example, and an opportunity to try out buoyancy aids, flippers and other equipment not normally allowed during public sessions at local pools. Ask at your local swimming pool for details of swimming clubs.

Being a competent swimmer opens up a host of other exciting possibilities, too. Sea swimming on holiday naturally becomes safer and much more enjoyable, and there are opportunities for trying other watersports — waterski-ing, windsurfing, scuba diving and canoeing to name just a few. But even if all you want from swimming is the ability to swim a few lengths of a pool for exercise, it is a skill you will always be glad to have. So why not get started today?

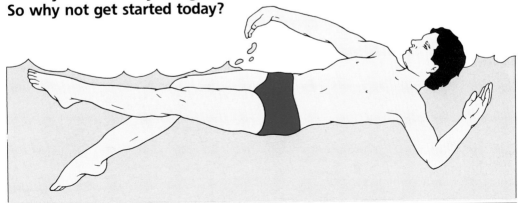

Equipment

Apart from a swimming costume or trunks, you don't actually need any other equipment to get started. But there are some useful buoyancy and other aids available.

Swimming trunks or costume

In a public pool you will need to be decent! Otherwise you can wear what you like, although there are sometimes rules for competitive swimming attire.

Hats

A rubber or lycra swimming hat is a useful accessory for swimmers with long hair, as a safety precaution as well as for comfort. In competitive swimming it can help reduce water resistance. Some pools insist on hats being worn.

Armbands

These ensure good support of the body with shoulders under the water and have the advantage of leaving your arms and legs free. You can gradually deflate them as you grow more confident.

Rubber ring

This can be reassuring as it allows you to get your feet off the bottom whilst keeping your head and shoulders well clear of the surface. Make sure it fits snugly under your arms, and try armbands instead as your confidence grows.

Equipment

Floats

These are effective buoyancy aids, and a number of different types are available. Once you are swimming, they are also useful as supports for practising leg and arm movements.

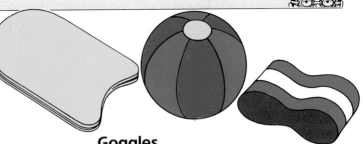

Goggles

Some swimmers like to use anti-chlorine goggles. These are not normally necessary for beginners but are useful for more advanced swimmers during long exposure to the water or for those with very sensitive eyes.

Ear plugs

These are helpful if you are prone to ear infections, which can be aggravated by water exposure.

Nose clip

Used in synchronised swimming when faces are under water for prolonged periods. Some beginners like them but they are not recommended – better to learn correct breathing techniques from the start.

Flippers

Flippers are useful once you are swimming for increasing your propulsion, particularly when swimming underwater. Not normally allowed at public pools.

Mask and snorkel

These are used for underwater swimming. Unlike goggles, the mask covers the nose and inhibits normal breathing. Not normally allowed in public pools but great fun for more experienced swimmers, especially in the sea.

Safety

When learning how to swim, it is extremely important that you are aware of the safety aspects at all times. These are mainly a matter of common sense, but be sure always to observe the safety rules and notices on display at pools, beaches and rivers. Remember: most swimming accidents are avoidable.

Your own safety

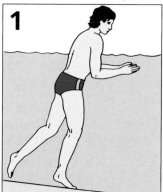

1

Keep within your own depth until you are a proficient swimmer.

2

In pools, keep well away from diving areas.

3

Don't run on the poolside — it can be very slippery.

4

At the seaside, never swim when the danger flags are flying.

5

Never swim alone.

Safety of others

Real life-saving requires a great deal of training and practice. If you are interested, lessons are offered at many swimming pools. However, there are some basic rules which even non-swimmers can observe if someone is in trouble.

1 Don't jump in the water to try to help someone if you cannot swim yourself or water conditions are difficult. Summon help if it is nearby.

2 Throw anything that will float for use as a life-float — a play ball, stick or any other floating object to hand.

3 Extend your reach towards the person in the water by throwing or reaching out with branches, poles, items of clothing or anything else that will cover the gap.

Health and Hygiene

● Don't swim in a public pool if you have a nose or ear infection.

● Do use the disinfected footbaths that are usually situated between the changing area and pool.

● Do take a short shower before as well as after your swim.

● Don't swim too soon after a meal — you will be liable to stomach cramps which can be dangerous.

● Do use a clean towel and launder your swim wear as often as any other items of clothing.

● Be particularly careful to dry thoroughly between your toes — conditions such as athlete's foot and verruccae are easily spread in wet conditions. If you do have a verrucca, do wear a rubber verrucca sock, readily available from chemists and some pools.

The Principles of Swimming

high floater

Flotation

Believe it or not, you *can* float without buoyancy aids! You may well be lower in the water than you expect and this could feel strange at first. Aim to keep your shoulders and arms underwater to give yourself maximum flotation. How high or low you float depends on the proportion of fat to muscle and bone in your body. Girls usually float higher than boys since their centre of buoyancy is lower. Relax and try it!

low floater

angled position increases resistance

Resistance

Stand in chest-high water and try to walk or run. This will show you how powerful the resistance of water can be. Your aim in swimming must be to reduce resistance as much as possible. Do this by learning to keep as flat as you can: try thinking of yourself as a streamlined torpedo.

body in streamlined position

Propulsion

You get your propulsion – or movement through the water – from using your arms and legs as levers and your hands and feet as paddles and propellers.

1 Newton's Law

Sir Isaac Newton's Third Law says that for every action there is an equal and opposite reaction. In swimming this means that if you push backwards with your hands, your body goes forward. If you want to stay up, you push down, and so on.

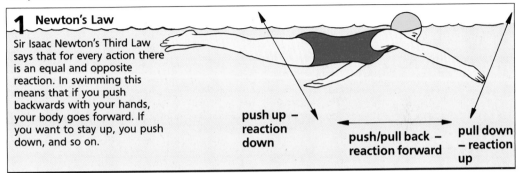

push up – reaction down

push/pull back – reaction forward

pull down – reaction up

2 Propeller Action

You also get movement from the flexibility in your hands and feet which act almost as propellers. This gives you a lift or thrust type of movement. Sculling illustrates the potential power of this: with your hands at 45° and thumbs up, push inwards, then outwards with your little finger up. Strong, practised sculling will produce a vortex like the one seen when you empty the bath.

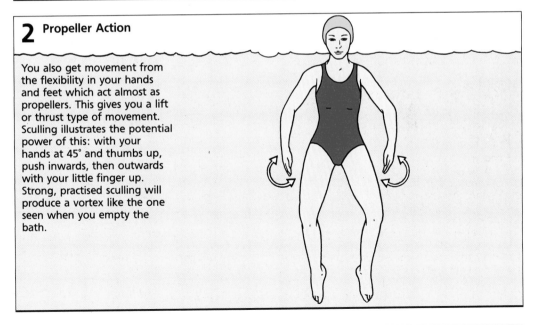

Gaining Confidence

If you are a beginner, just being in the water may be a little unnerving at first. Here are some simple exercises to get you started and increase confidence.

Remember not to get out of your depth and, above all, relax and enjoy yourself. (If you are already swimming, you can skip this section if you like).

1 Walking

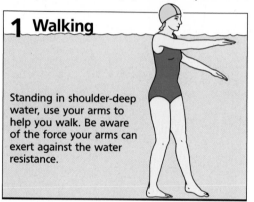

Standing in shoulder-deep water, use your arms to help you walk. Be aware of the force your arms can exert against the water resistance.

2 Blowing bubbles

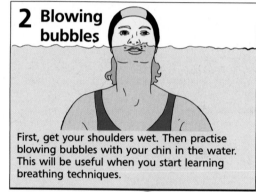

First, get your shoulders wet. Then practise blowing bubbles with your chin in the water. This will be useful when you start learning breathing techniques.

3 Shallow water

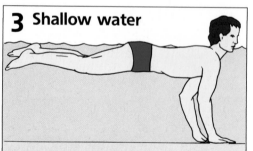

Not all pools are shallow enough, but if you can, put your hands on the bottom and raise your body to the surface. Then try 'walking' along on your hands. You can gradually introduce a paddle motion to reduce the support.

4 Jumping

Jumping up and down in the water is not only enjoyable but helps with balance and confidence. Jumping into the pool from the side is a good progression.

5 Treading water

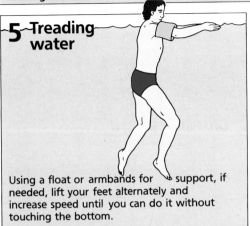

Using a float or armbands for support, if needed, lift your feet alternately and increase speed until you can do it without touching the bottom.

6 Regaining standing position

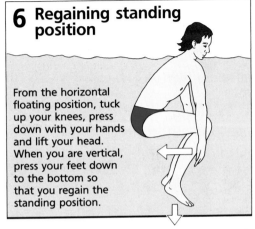

From the horizontal floating position, tuck up your knees, press down with your hands and lift your head. When you are vertical, press your feet down to the bottom so that you regain the standing position.

7 Floats – forwards

Hold a float out flat in front of you and, with shoulders under, walk forward. Now try leaning forwards into the swimming position.

8 Floats – backwards

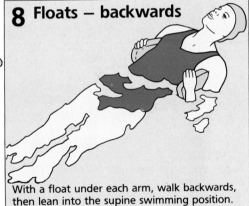

With a float under each arm, walk backwards, then lean into the supine swimming position.

Once you've got your feet up and are moving through the water, even if only with a 'dog paddle' stroke, you are well on the way to proficient swimming. It is at this stage that you will most benefit from some professional lessons, and can work on the stroke techniques in the following sections.

Breast Stroke

In 1875 Matthew Webb used breast stroke to become the first person to swim the English Channel. Breast stroke is a popular choice for beginners for two main reasons. First, since your head can be held out of the water, breathing is not a problem. And second, you are in a prone position which allows you to see where you are going.

It is a good stroke for building up confidence, but it is also the slowest competitive stroke. This is because the movements are less continuous than in the crawl strokes, and because the arms and legs recover under water and cause resistance.

Body position

1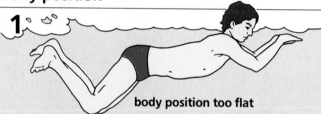

body position too flat

Keep your body as horizontal as possible. In fact, it will be slightly inclined downwards since the leg action takes place under water. If you try to lie too flat, your feet will break the surface.

2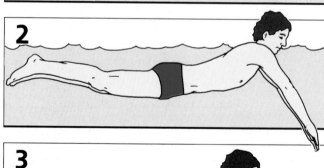

Aim to be as streamlined as possible. When your arms are pulling, your legs should trail straight behind.

3

Similarly, while your leg action is taking place, make sure your arm recovery and extension is as streamlined as possible.

Leg action

There are two quite distinct types of leg action, the wedge kick and the whip kick.

Wedge kick

Used mainly by beginners, the old-fashioned wedge kick is alright for recreation but not very efficient. It gives a slower tempo for a more relaxed stroke.

From the extended position, draw your feet up towards your bottom. Your knees move forward and out, heels almost touching (diagrams 1 and 2).

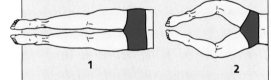

Now push your legs out, back and in with a sweeping movement. Your heels lead, with toes turned towards your shin and soles facing backwards. As your feet and legs move backwards, the movement gains speed (diagrams 3, 4 and 5).

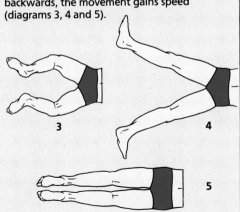

Whip kick

This is a much more mechanically efficient and streamlined action, used by competitive swimmers and adopted quite naturally by many beginners.

From the extended position, draw your knees up towards your bottom, about hip width apart. Your thighs make an angle of about 120-130° with your body. Seen from behind, you look rather like a letter 'W'. Your knee width can vary. Your feet turn outward, soles facing up (diagrams 1, 2 and 3).

Now push out and back with your feet so they come together in a smooth, powerful, curving movement. The thrust starts with a whip-like action from the inner sides of your feet. Think of your feet as broad paddles driving you forward as you extend your legs (diagrams 4 and 5).

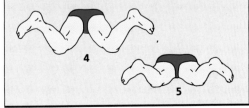

Arm action

All the arm movements in breast stroke must be under water. The arms move simultaneously and continuously in a circular motion, except for a short glide. Catch point should be early. In the glide position, have your thumbs touching and little fingers raised so that your palms face out and down. This is not the only possible position, but it raises your elbows to give you more propulsive power on the pull phase.

There are two main types of arm action, the straight arm pull and the bent arm pull.

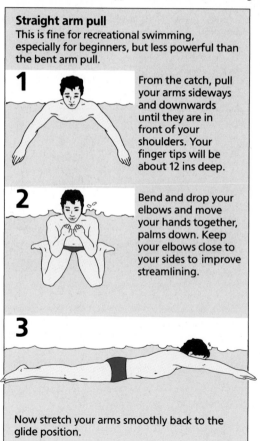

Straight arm pull

This is fine for recreational swimming, especially for beginners, but less powerful than the bent arm pull.

1 From the catch, pull your arms sideways and downwards until they are in front of your shoulders. Your finger tips will be about 12 ins deep.

2 Bend and drop your elbows and move your hands together, palms down. Keep your elbows close to your sides to improve streamlining.

3

Now stretch your arms smoothly back to the glide position.

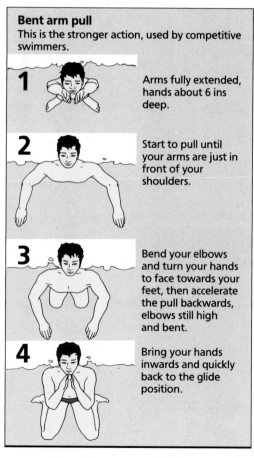

Bent arm pull

This is the stronger action, used by competitive swimmers.

1 Arms fully extended, hands about 6 ins deep.

2 Start to pull until your arms are just in front of your shoulders.

3 Bend your elbows and turn your hands to face towards your feet, then accelerate the pull backwards, elbows still high and bent.

4 Bring your hands inwards and quickly back to the glide position.

Breathing and timing

Because your face is out of the water, breathing in breast stroke is not a problem, but you should remember to breathe regularly and not hold your breath. The best time to take a breath is at the end of the pull phase.

Once you have mastered the individual elements, combining the actions of your arms, legs and breathing will come fairly naturally. It helps to think of the sequence 'pull-breathe-kick-glide'.

Inverted Breast Stroke

Otherwise known as 'elementary back stroke', inverted breast stroke is not only enjoyable in its own right, it is also excellent practice for your breast stroke leg action, and particularly helpful for correcting an uneven or 'screw' kick. It is also a useful life-saving and survival stroke.

2 Leg action

Your legs provide the propulsion and keep you in a good position. It is basically a breast stroke kick. Keep your feet turned out and ankles bent so the soles of your feet make the kick. At the end of the kick you can hold a glide if you like.

1 Body position

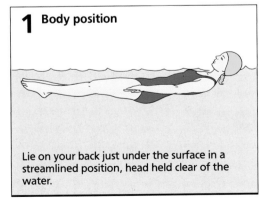

Lie on your back just under the surface in a streamlined position, head held clear of the water.

3 Arm action

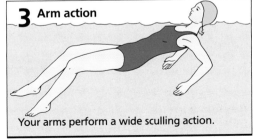

Your arms perform a wide sculling action.

Breast Stroke Sequence

**The sequence outlined here shows the more efficient whip kick and bent arm actions.
Remember the sequence: pull-breathe-kick-glide, pull-breathe-kick-glide.**

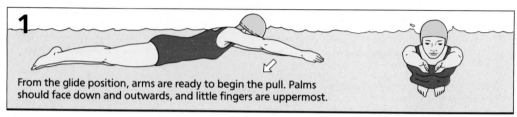

1

From the glide position, arms are ready to begin the pull. Palms
should face down and outwards, and little fingers are uppermost.

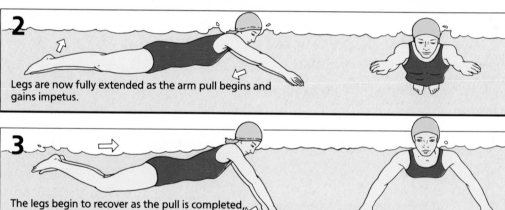

2

Legs are now fully extended as the arm pull begins and
gains impetus.

3

The legs begin to recover as the pull is completed,
and a breath is taken.

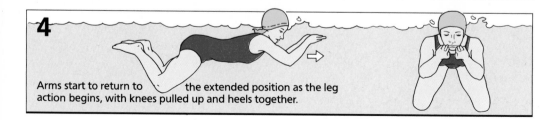

4

Arms start to return to   the extended position as the leg
action begins, with knees pulled up and heels together.

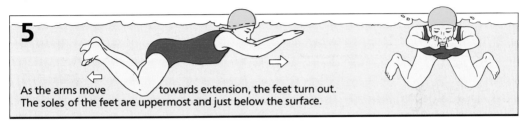

5 As the arms move   towards extension, the feet turn out.
The soles of the feet are uppermost and just below the surface.

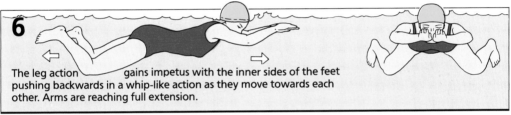

6 The leg action   gains impetus with the inner sides of the feet
pushing backwards in a whip-like action as they move towards each
other. Arms are reaching full extension.

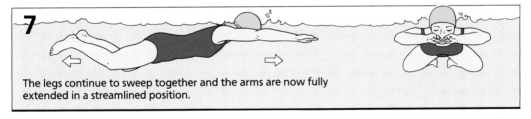

7 The legs continue to sweep together and the arms are now fully
extended in a streamlined position.

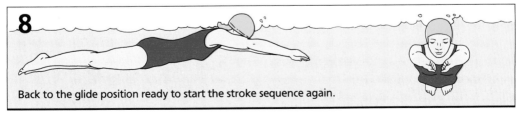

8 Back to the glide position ready to start the stroke sequence again.

Breast Stroke Practice

These practice exercises will help you to improve your breast stroke technique and build up your strength — once you have mastered the basic stroke.

Arms

1

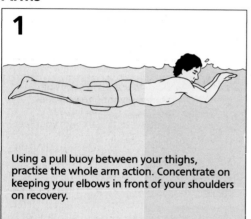

Using a pull buoy between your thighs, practise the whole arm action. Concentrate on keeping your elbows in front of your shoulders on recovery.

2

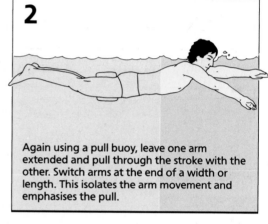

Again using a pull buoy, leave one arm extended and pull through the stroke with the other. Switch arms at the end of a width or length. This isolates the arm movement and emphasises the pull.

3

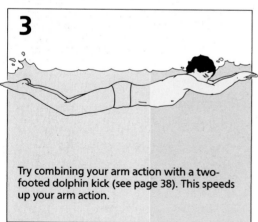

Try combining your arm action with a two-footed dolphin kick (see page 38). This speeds up your arm action.

4

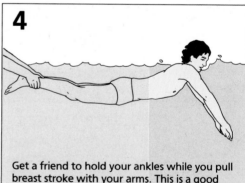

Get a friend to hold your ankles while you pull breast stroke with your arms. This is a good resistance exercise for strengthening your arm action.

Legs

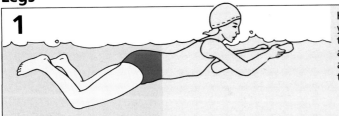

1 Holding a kickboard, and with your head raised and chin out of the water, practise your leg action only. You can change the angle of the kickboard to vary the level of resistance.

2 Hold your arms at your sides, fingers pointing to your feet. Now with each leg recovery, touch your fingers with your feet before kicking back on the propulsive phase. This helps give good body position and keeps your knees narrower.

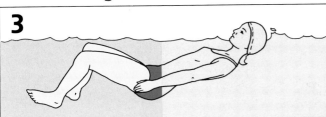

3 Push off on your back and kick using inverted breast stroke (see page 31). Keep your head up so that your knees stay under. This is useful because you can watch your legs and correct any faults.

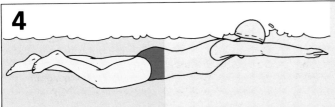

4 Kick with an 'eggbeater' motion — that is, using your legs alternately instead of together. This is good for strengthening your kick and isolating the leg movement.

Front Crawl

Front crawl — or freestyle — is the fastest and most efficient stroke and is sometimes the first stroke learned as it is a natural progression from 'dog-paddle'. Basically, you are on your front in a horizontal streamlined position, your legs under the water kicking

Body position

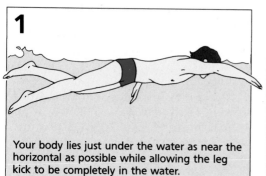

1

Your body lies just under the water as near the horizontal as possible while allowing the leg kick to be completely in the water.

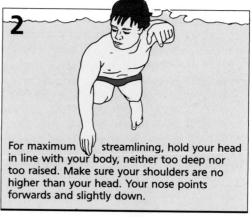

2

For maximum streamlining, hold your head in line with your body, neither too deep nor too raised. Make sure your shoulders are no higher than your head. Your nose points forwards and slightly down.

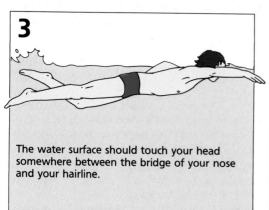

3

The water surface should touch your head somewhere between the bridge of your nose and your hairline.

4

up to 70° roll

Your body should roll naturally as you swim. Don't try to do this consciously as you will increase resistance. The amount of roll will vary according to your physique and technique.

alternately up and down with pointed toes. Your arms also move alternately but come out of the water for recovery. Your face is in the water and turns to the side for breathing.

When learning this or any other stroke, your movements will be based on instinct to some extent at first. You then need to analyse the stroke, work on the separate elements and, finally, put it all back together again.

Leg action

Although your leg kick gives some propulsion, its main function is to help you maintain a balanced, streamlined swimming position. It should be a relaxed, supple movement.

1

Kick your legs alternately *from your hips*, with knees slightly flexed, legs passing close together. Although basically an up and down action, don't try to keep your legs completely in the vertical plane – just let them move with the body roll.

2

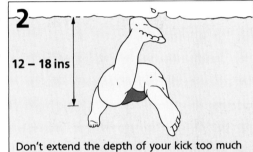

12 – 18 ins

Don't extend the depth of your kick too much – probably no more than 12-18 ins below the surface.

3

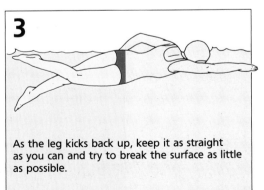

As the leg kicks back up, keep it as straight as you can and try to break the surface as little as possible.

4

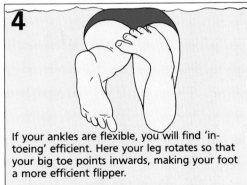

If your ankles are flexible, you will find 'in-toeing' efficient. Here your leg rotates so that your big toe points inwards, making your foot a more efficient flipper.

Arm action

The arm action is what really gets you moving forward, and it consists of four distinct stages blending into one alternating, continuous movement.

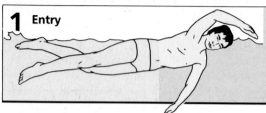

1 Entry

Imagine a line forward from the middle of your head and another extending from your shoulder. Your hand enters the water, fingers first, between these two lines. Your elbow should be slightly flexed, and higher than your hand.

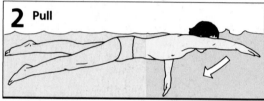

2 Pull

Just under the water is the 'catch point' where your hand starts to exert downward and backward pressure. Think of your arm as a lever – you will get maximum power if your wrist is firm, your elbow bent and your fingers either together or *slightly* parted.

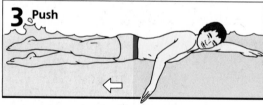

3 Push

Follow the movement right through by pressing your hand backwards under your body towards your thigh until you feel your thumb brush your leg. Your elbow is much straighter now.

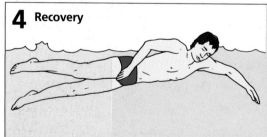

4 Recovery

Now come out of the water ready for the next stroke. You can do this in either of two ways. Either lift your elbow high and, keeping your hand relaxed and fingers just above the surface, bring your hand forward (see diagram). Or, with your elbow much less flexed, swing your arm forward in a large semi-circle with your little finger upwards and the back of your hand facing forward. This is less streamlined than the first method.

Breathing

You might find it helpful to swim with held breath at first so as to concentrate on your leg and arm actions. But you should learn to breathe effectively once you have mastered the basic stroke. Breathing needs to be smoothly incorporated into your stroke to impede it as little as possible. In front crawl you breathe as one hand is forward at the catch and the other just leaving the water.

You can breathe to the right or the left. It is an advantage to learn both sides, which gives you the flexibility to breathe every one and a half strokes (known as bi-lateral breathing). It will help the balance of your roll and is useful in speed swimming, enabling you to keep an eye on other competitors when racing.

1 Turn your head — don't lift it — towards your chosen side as that arm completes its action and begins recovery. Open your mouth wide and push out your breath explosively. Some air will be released under the water, some above.

Breathe in. You won't need to turn your head very much because there is a 'trough' immediately behind the wave created by your head as it moves through the water, and you breathe in from this.

3 Return your head to the front as the recovering arm is carried forward and hold your breath again ready for the next stroke.

4 Instead of an explosive out-breath, you can try expelling the air gradually through your mouth and nose while your face is submerged. Then inhale quickly as your mouth clears the water. This is called 'trickle breathing'.

Front Crawl Sequence

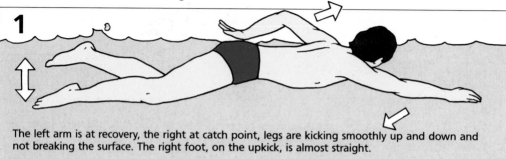

1

The left arm is at recovery, the right at catch point, legs are kicking smoothly up and down and not breaking the surface. The right foot, on the upkick, is almost straight.

2

The right arm accelerates into the pull as the left arm recovers. The right knee flexes to begin a downkick.

3

The right arm begins the backwards and upwards push as the left arm enters the water.

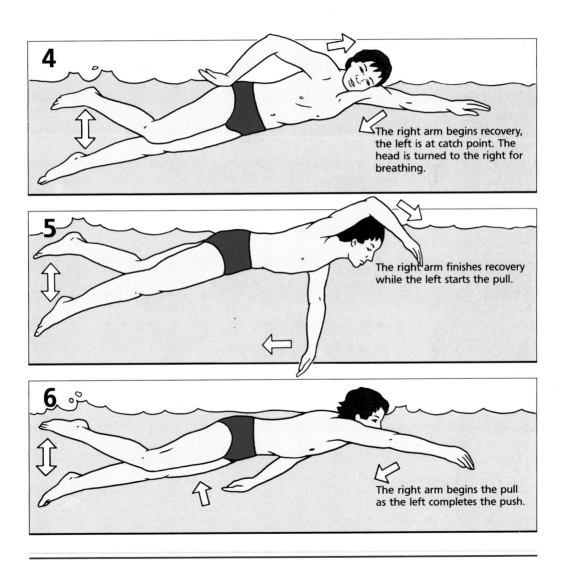

4 The right arm begins recovery, the left is at catch point. The head is turned to the right for breathing.

5 The right arm finishes recovery while the left starts the pull.

6 The right arm begins the pull as the left completes the push.

Front Crawl Practice

These practice exercises (and those given for the other strokes later in the book) are slightly more advanced and will help improve the strength and technique of your strokes. It is a good idea to join a swimming club as many accept beginners, and you will be able to use equipment such as flippers and floats which are not normally allowed during public sessions.

Arms

1

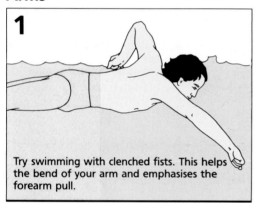

Try swimming with clenched fists. This helps the bend of your arm and emphasises the forearm pull.

2

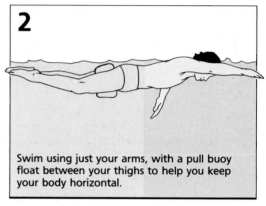

Swim using just your arms, with a pull buoy float between your thighs to help you keep your body horizontal.

3

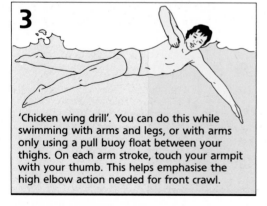

'Chicken wing drill'. You can do this while swimming with arms and legs, or with arms only using a pull buoy float between your thighs. On each arm stroke, touch your armpit with your thumb. This helps emphasise the high elbow action needed for front crawl.

4

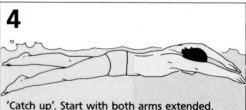

'Catch up'. Start with both arms extended. Push off from the wall and kick hard. Now use one arm only for several strokes, bringing it back each time to the other extended arm. Repeat with the other arm. This gives a good feel for the catch point and push/pull phases of the stroke.

Legs

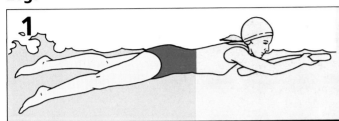

Holding a float, practise your front crawl kicks only. This can be done with your head raised or with a selected breathing pattern. It is a good general conditioning exercise.

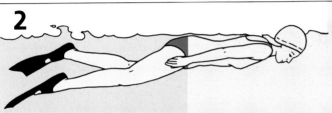

Try kicking with flippers. You can do this with your arms either extended or at your sides. Flippers help build up strength in your legs and increase the suppleness of the ankles.

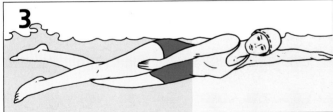

Kick to the side, with one arm pointing to the front and your face resting on your shoulder. Keep your other hand at the side, pointing backwards. Try to do a length, then swap sides.

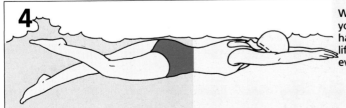

With your face down, extend your arms and overlap your hands. Now practise your kick, lifting your head to breathe on every sixth kick.

Back Crawl

There are several ways of swimming on your back, of which back crawl is one (another popular stroke, the inverted breast stroke, is described on page 33). Swimming on your back is comparatively restful, since your face is clear of the water. The main disadvantage is that you cannot see where you are going, and you'll need to be careful to avoid collisions, especially in a busy pool.

Back crawl consists of an alternating leg kick and alternating arm action with overwater recovery.

Body position

1

Viewed from the side, try to imagine your body in a streamlined 'shallow dish' shape.

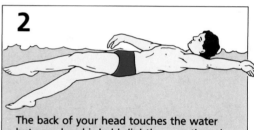

2

The back of your head touches the water but your head is held slightly up as though supported by a cushion (not too high or your feet will drop). The water line should be around your ears.

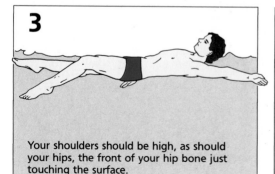

3

Your shoulders should be high, as should your hips, the front of your hip bone just touching the surface.

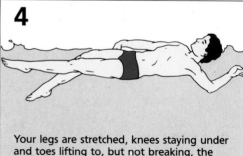

4

Your legs are stretched, knees staying under and toes lifting to, but not breaking, the surface.

Leg action

An effective leg kick is essential in back crawl, and you should master this before trying the arm action. Its main purpose is to stabilize and maintain a good body position.

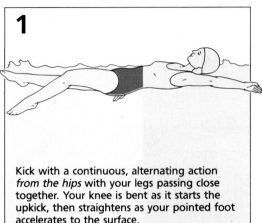

1

Kick with a continuous, alternating action *from the hips* with your legs passing close together. Your knee is bent as it starts the upkick, then straightens as your pointed foot accelerates to the surface.

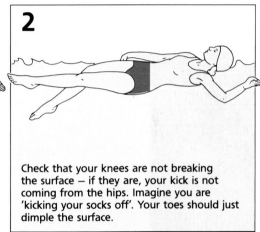

2

Check that your knees are not breaking the surface — if they are, your kick is not coming from the hips. Imagine you are 'kicking your socks off'. Your toes should just dimple the surface.

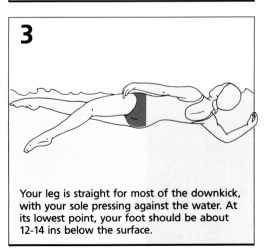

3

Your leg is straight for most of the downkick, with your sole pressing against the water. At its lowest point, your foot should be about 12-14 ins below the surface.

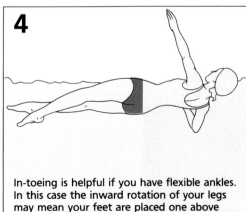

4

In-toeing is helpful if you have flexible ankles. In this case the inward rotation of your legs may mean your feet are placed one above the other rather than side by side.

Arm action

There are two possible extremes of arm action in back crawl: one with bent arms (sometimes known as 'S' pull) and one with straight arms. The bent arm action is more efficient and powerful and is outlined below.

1 Entry

Entry can be in line with, or slightly wide of, your shoulders, but try to get as close as you can to your centre line. Your arm should be stretched but not stiff. Your little finger should enter the water first as the arm brushes your ear. Let your body roll naturally, but remember to keep your head still.

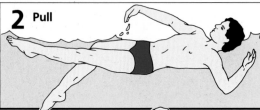

2 Pull

Turn your hand early and try to press down before catch point at about 6 ins below the surface. Your elbow starts to bend and your arm rotates until your hand is level with your elbow.

3 Push

When your shoulder, hand and elbow are level, they are ready to give a powerful push towards the bottom of the pool. Keep your hand facing down towards your feet until your arm is fully stretched.

Your hand will have traced a pattern rather like the letter 'S'.

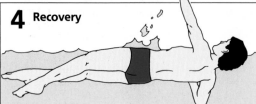

4 Recovery

Lift your straight arm from the water, vertically, and swing it smoothly back to entry position. Again, your body should roll to help reduce resistance.

Breathing

Because your head is out of the water, you probably won't need to think too much about breathing at first. But do get into the habit of breathing regularly and avoid holding your breath. A good rhythm to develop is to inhale on the recovery of one arm and exhale on the recovery of the other. Breathe in through your nose and out through your mouth and nose.

Timing

The correct timing of the arms and legs will come naturally as a result of the action-reaction pattern. It is useful to be aware of how this happens.

During the second part of the pull phase, your hand action pulls your hips to that side. To compensate, your opposite leg automatically kicks diagonally upward and inward.

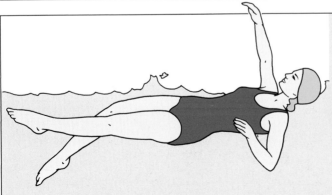

This action-reaction pattern means that you should instinctively develop a six-beat cycle: six flutter kicks for every complete arm cycle, or three for each arm. To check, concentrate on either hand as it enters the water. It should be balanced by the opposite leg with the toes just popping up.

Back Crawl Sequence

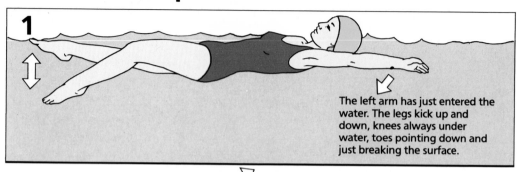

1

The left arm has just entered the water. The legs kick up and down, knees always under water, toes pointing down and just breaking the surface.

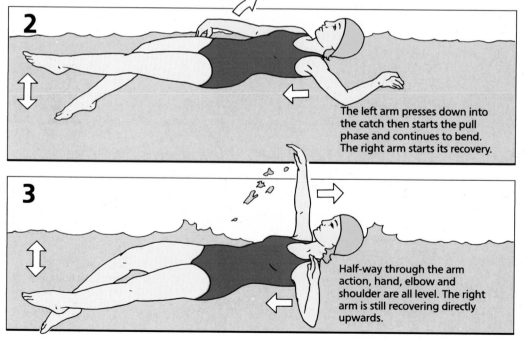

2

The left arm presses down into the catch then starts the pull phase and continues to bend. The right arm starts its recovery.

3

Half-way through the arm action, hand, elbow and shoulder are all level. The right arm is still recovering directly upwards.

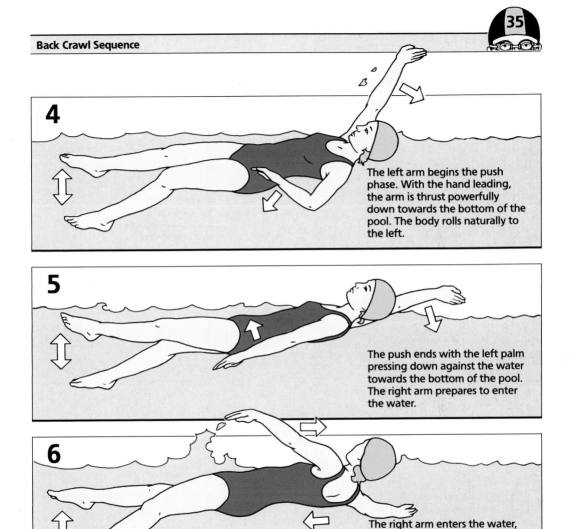

4

The left arm begins the push phase. With the hand leading, the arm is thrust powerfully down towards the bottom of the pool. The body rolls naturally to the left.

5

The push ends with the left palm pressing down against the water towards the bottom of the pool. The right arm prepares to enter the water.

6

The right arm enters the water, little finger first. As the body rolls to the right, the left foot kicks upwards to compensate and maintain the streamlined position.

Back Crawl Practice

Once your have mastered the basic stroke, try these exercises to improve your strength and technique.

Arms

1

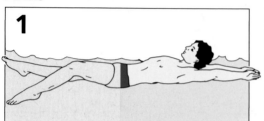

'Catch up stroke'. Push off with both arms extended above your head. Kick six times then pull strongly with your right arm through the stroke and back to join the other extended arm. Change to the left arm on touching hands. This improves flexibility and positioning of your hand as it enters behind your head.

2

With a pull buoy float between your thighs to help you keep your body horizontal, practise your arms only.

3

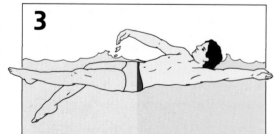

'Single arm stroke'. Keep one arm extended while the other goes through the stroke. Keep it up for a length if possible, then swap arms. This is very good for developing the full stroking rhythm and the shoulder lift in the recovery phase.

4

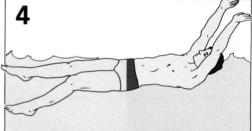

For a variation on single arm swimming try doing two strokes with your left arm, then two with your right, then two double arm pulls, returning after each pair of strokes to full extension of your arms above your head.

Legs

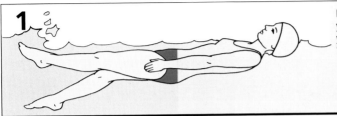

Practise kicking with your arms at your sides. Concentrate on letting your toes just break the surface: 'make the water boil'.

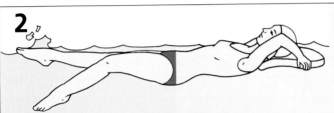

Hold a kickboard float behind your head to support it in a 'pillow' position. Then practise your leg action, again concentrating on just breaking the surface with your toes.

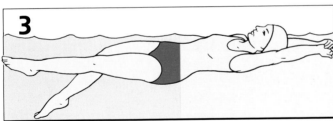

Extend both arms above your head, clasp your hands together and try to rest your head on your upper arms. Now practise kicking. This is very good for emphasising the body's natural roll.

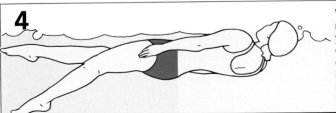

With your hands at your sides, roll onto your right side, raising your left shoulder and elbow clear of the water. After six kicks, change sides. This again introduces the body's rolling motion and also helps the shoulder to clear before recovery.

Butterfly

This is the newest of the four competitive strokes. It is an impressive, elegant and powerful stroke. Although not as difficult as is sometimes thought beginners will find it the hardest of the strokes to master. Your body moves in a continuous, rhythmic, up-and-down movement not unlike the motion of a dolphin.

Body position

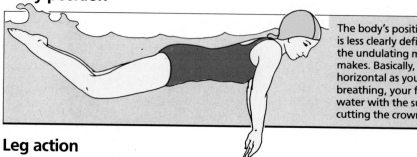

The body's position in the water is less clearly defined because of the undulating movements it makes. Basically, try to keep as horizontal as you can. When not breathing, your face is in the water with the surface line cutting the crown.

Leg action

The legs kick simultaneously up and down, balancing the arm and body movements and causing the undulating movements characteristic of the stroke. Two kicks are completed for every arm cycle. Think of the sequence 'kick-pull-kick-throw'.

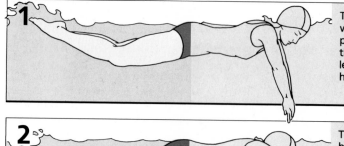

1 The upkick comes from the hips, with the soles of your feet pressing up and back through the water. Start with straight legs: your knees bend as your hips start to drop.

2 Thrust down again from the hips. At the end of the downkick your legs are fully extended and about 20-24 ins deep.

Arm action

1 Entry

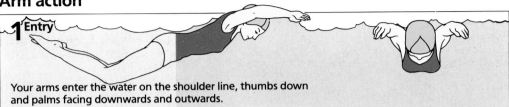

Your arms enter the water on the shoulder line, thumbs down and palms facing downwards and outwards.

2 Pull – outsweep

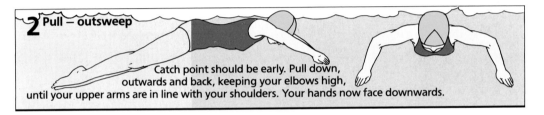

Catch point should be early. Pull down, outwards and back, keeping your elbows high, until your upper arms are in line with your shoulders. Your hands now face downwards.

3 Pull – insweep

Accelerate your hands inwards toward each other, changing the pitch of your hands from outwards to inwards as you do so.

4 Push

Now with hands facing your feet, push outward, upward and backward for the final thrust.

5 Recovery

Hands and arms leave the water palms up. You then 'throw' them just above the surface, sideways and forwards for the next stroke.

Breathing

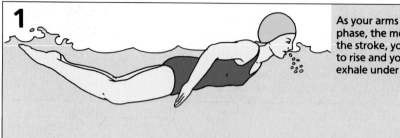

1 As your arms complete the push phase, the most powerful part of the stroke, your shoulders begin to rise and you can start to exhale under water.

2 During the early part of your arm recovery, as your mouth clears the surface, continue to breathe out explosively, then quickly breathe in before lowering your head again as your hands enter the water for the catch phase.

Butterfly Sequence

Timing and co-ordination are vital in the butterfly stroke. Remember: kick-pull-kick-throw.

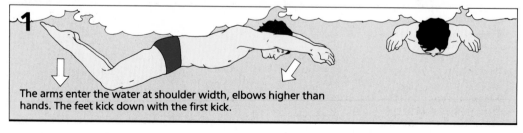

1 The arms enter the water at shoulder width, elbows higher than hands. The feet kick down with the first kick.

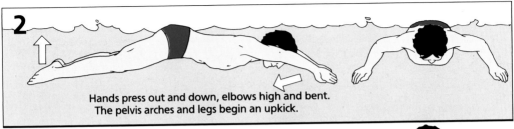

2 Hands press out and down, elbows high and bent. The pelvis arches and legs begin an upkick.

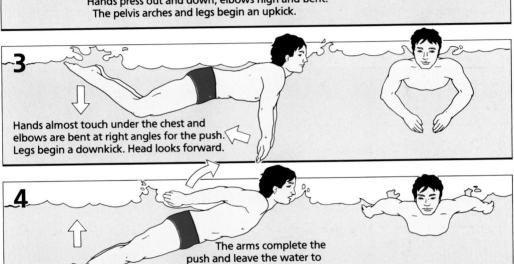

3 Hands almost touch under the chest and elbows are bent at right angles for the push. Legs begin a downkick. Head looks forward.

4 The arms complete the push and leave the water to begin recovery. The legs are at their deepest point. Breathe in.

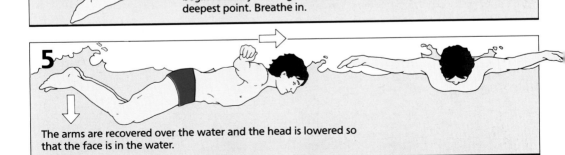

5 The arms are recovered over the water and the head is lowered so that the face is in the water.

Butterfly Practice

When you have mastered the butterfly technique, and thus the most difficult of all the swimming strokes, you can further improve your style and agility with these exercises.

Arms

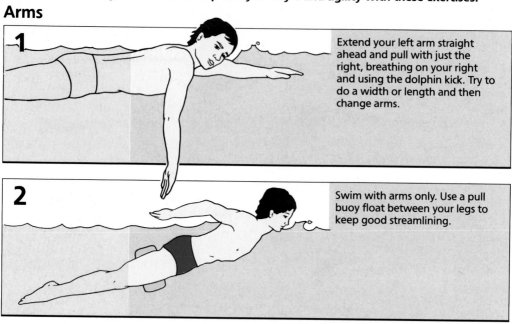

1 Extend your left arm straight ahead and pull with just the right, breathing on your right and using the dolphin kick. Try to do a width or length and then change arms.

2 Swim with arms only. Use a pull buoy float between your legs to keep good streamlining.

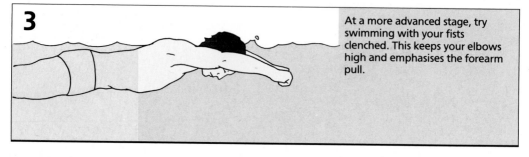

3 At a more advanced stage, try swimming with your fists clenched. This keeps your elbows high and emphasises the forearm pull.

Legs

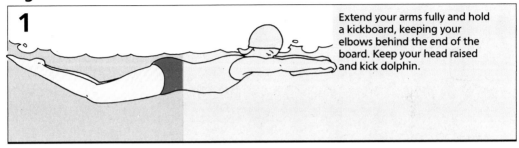

1 Extend your arms fully and hold a kickboard, keeping your elbows behind the end of the board. Keep your head raised and kick dolphin.

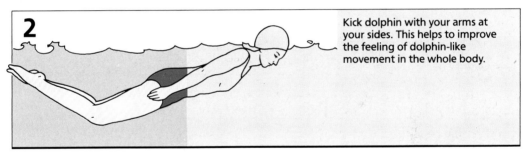

2 Kick dolphin with your arms at your sides. This helps to improve the feeling of dolphin-like movement in the whole body.

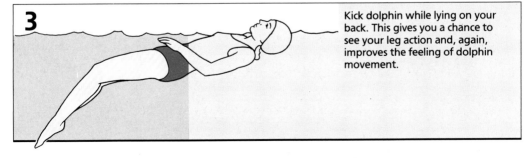

3 Kick dolphin while lying on your back. This gives you a chance to see your leg action and, again, improves the feeling of dolphin movement.

DEVELOPING YOUR SKILLS

Diving Basics

Diving is great fun. But before you try diving in head first from the poolside, make sure you can:

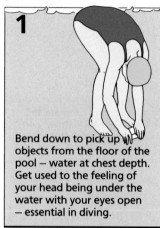

1 Bend down to pick up objects from the floor of the pool — water at chest depth. Get used to the feeling of your head being under the water with your eyes open — essential in diving.

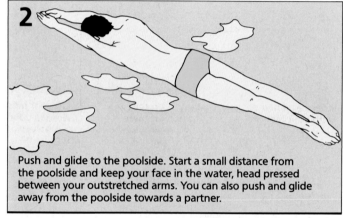

2 Push and glide to the poolside. Start a small distance from the poolside and keep your face in the water, head pressed between your outstretched arms. You can also push and glide away from the poolside towards a partner.

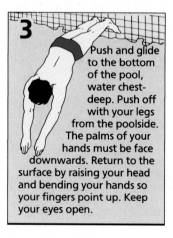

3 Push and glide to the bottom of the pool, water chest-deep. Push off with your legs from the poolside. The palms of your hands must be face downwards. Return to the surface by raising your head and bending your hands so your fingers point up. Keep your eyes open.

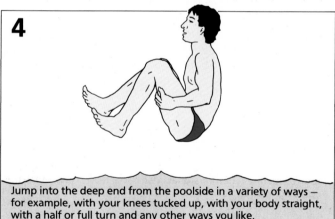

4 Jump into the deep end from the poolside in a variety of ways — for example, with your knees tucked up, with your body straight, with a half or full turn and any other ways you like.

Sitting dive

This is a very shallow dive but even so should not be attempted in very shallow water.

Knees together or slightly apart, sit on the side with your feet on the rail or trough (if there isn't one, don't try a sitting dive). Stretch out your arms, with one hand on top of the other, palms down. The top of your head should point towards the water.

Lift your hips and push off. Your arms are still close to your head. Keep your head down and stretch out in a straight line towards the bottom of the pool.

Lunge dive

This is a shallow dive but, again, don't attempt it in extremely shallow water.

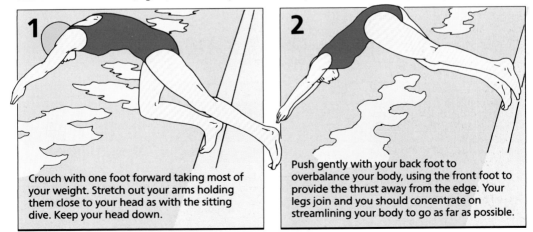

Crouch with one foot forward taking most of your weight. Stretch out your arms holding them close to your head as with the sitting dive. Keep your head down.

Push gently with your back foot to overbalance your body, using the front foot to provide the thrust away from the edge. Your legs join and you should concentrate on streamlining your body to go as far as possible.

The plain header

This is the most useful preliminary dive and is relatively easy to learn. Water should be at least eight feet deep — deeper if you are going off a diving board.

1 Ready position

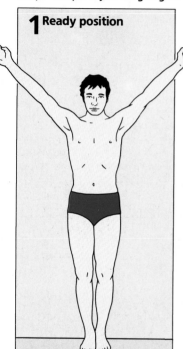

Stand on the poolside, your toes gripping the edge and your heels touching. Bring your arms up in a 'V', in line with your body, palms forward and fingers closed. Look at a point far away just above your head.

2 Take-off

Bend your knees slightly and move your shoulders forward a little, shifting your weight onto the balls of your feet. Then push off vigorously, straightening your knees quickly. The push should come upwards through your hips. Be careful to keep your arms in line with your body — they shouldn't move forward and downwards at all.

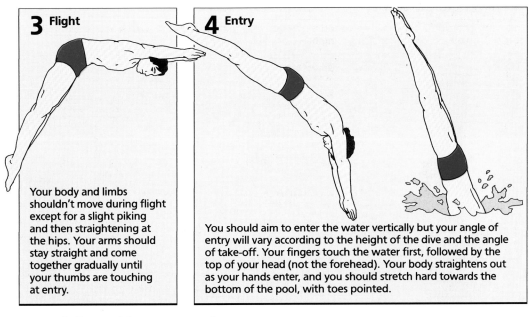

3 Flight

4 Entry

Your body and limbs shouldn't move during flight except for a slight piking and then straightening at the hips. Your arms should stay straight and come together gradually until your thumbs are touching at entry.

You should aim to enter the water vertically but your angle of entry will vary according to the height of the dive and the angle of take-off. Your fingers touch the water first, followed by the top of your head (not the forehead). Your body straightens out as your hands enter, and you should stretch hard towards the bottom of the pool, with toes pointed.

Looking Forward

Once you have mastered the basic strokes and simple dives, you may wish to develop your swimming skills further. As noted earlier, one of the best ways to progress is to join a club, or take some professional lessons. So what comes next?

● **Starts and turns**
Although mainly associated with competitive swimming, the ability to perform good starts and turns will be a useful and satisfying addition to your swimming skills.

● **Advanced diving**
Diving is an exciting and rewarding speciality much enjoyed by many enthusiasts.

● **Underwater swimming**
● **Lifesaving techniques**
● **Specialist water sports**
Such as scuba diving, water polo, synchronised swimming and canoeing.

Glossary

ACTION In swimming, any movement of the limbs. For every action there is an equal and opposite reaction (see page 11).

CATCH The point directly after entry at which the hands begin to exert pressure on the water.

DOG-PADDLE A very basic, instinctive, prone swimming stroke which uses an alternating crawl-style leg kick and an alternating arm action with an underwater recovery.

DOLPHIN KICK Double leg kick used for the butterfly stroke.

EARLY BREATHING Breathing before the optimum moment (see LATE BREATHING).

GLIDE POSITION A streamlined body position, with arms stretched above and close to the head; a glide can be performed on the front or the back, on the surface or under water.

IN-TOEING Inward rotation of the legs, giving greater foot extension and making the foot a more efficient paddle.

KICKBOARD Another name for a float, usually held in the hands for practising leg action.

LATE BREATHING Breathing after the optimum moment (see EARLY BREATHING).

PIKING A position adopted during the flight of some dives with the body bent forward from the hips and head and arms pointing down.

PRONE Swimming position with the body on its front.

PULL The phase of a stroke where the arm first accelerates to give maximum propulsion. The pull ends at the shoulder.

PULL BUOY A type of shaped float usually held between the legs when practising arm action.

PUSH The phase of a stroke where the arm continues to exert pressure past the shoulder.

RECOVERY The phase of a stroke during which the limbs are returned to the position from which they started.

'S' PULL An efficient back crawl arm action which describes the shape of a letter 'S' under water.

SCREW KICK An uneven leg kick in breast stoke.

SCULLING Propulsion caused by small, twisting, hand movement (see page 11).

SUPINE Swimming position with the body on its back.

TRICKLE BREATHING Allowing exhaled breath to escape gradually rather than explosively.

WEDGE KICK Inefficient breast stroke leg action where the soles of the feet face backwards or partly backwards, a poor position for thrust.

WHIP KICK Efficient, narrow-action breast stroke kick where the soles of the feet face upwards for maximum thrust.

Printed in Italy